BEST OF JOHN DENVER

Silver Anniversary Edition

EASY GUITAR

T0088541

2	Annie's Song
4	Back Home Again
7	Calypso
10	Eagles And Horses (I'm Flying Again)
13	Fly Away
16	Follow Me
19	Leaving On A Jet Plane
22	For Baby (For Bobbie)
24	For You
27	Looking For Space
30	Grandma's Feather Bed
32	I'm Sorry
34	My Sweet Lady
36	Never A Doubt
40	Perhaps Love
42	Poems, Prayers And Promises
46	Goodbye Again
49	Rocky Mountain High
52	Sunshine On My Shoulders
54	Take Me Home, Country Roads
57	Whispering Jesse
60	Thank God I'm A Country Boy
62	Wild Montana Skies

Management: Advent Management Corp.
Production: Daniel Rosenbaum/Rana Bernhardt
Art Direction: Rosemary Cappa-Jenkins
Director of Music: Mark Phillips

Photography by John Russell

Annie's Song

Words and Music by
John Denver

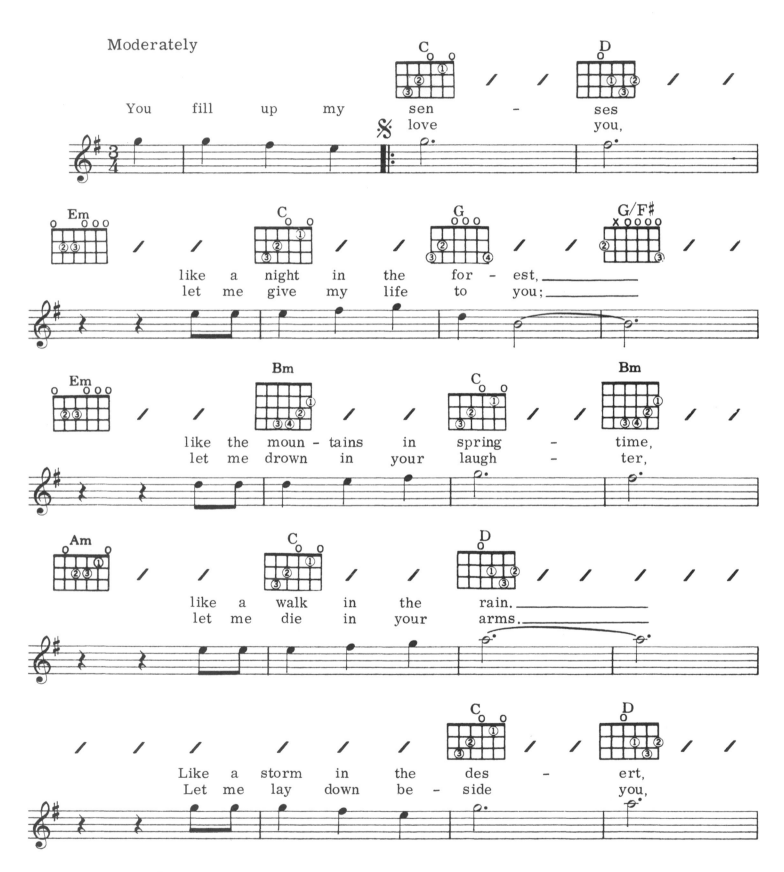

like a sleep-y blue o-cean,_____
let me al-ways be with you;_____

you fill up my sen - ses,
come let me love you,

come fill me a - gain._____
come love me a - gain._____

To Coda

1. Come let me

2. You fill up my

D. S. (lyric 1) al Coda 𝄋

Coda
gain.

Back Home Again

Words and Music by
John Denver

D7

ten days on the road____ are bare-ly gone._____ There's a
what's the lat-est thing____ the neigh-bors say?_____ And your
lit-tle things that make____ a house a home._____ Like a

G7   **C**

fire___ soft-ly burn-ing   sup-per's on the stove___ But it's the
moth-er called last Fri-day;   "Sun-shine" made her cry,____ And you
fire___ soft-ly burn-ing   and sup-per on the stove___ And the

D7   **G**

light in your eyes that makes him warm._____
felt the ba-by move just yes-ter-day._____
light in your eyes that makes me warm._____

Chorus

C   **D7**   **G**   **G7**

Hey, it's good to be back home a-gain;_____

C   **D7**   **G**

Some-times this old farm feels like a long-lost

5

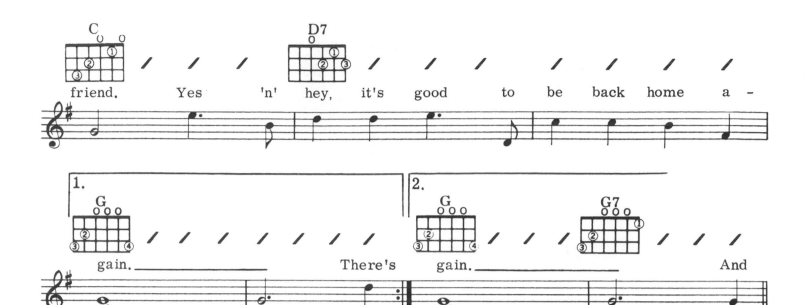

friend. Yes 'n' hey, it's good to be back home a-

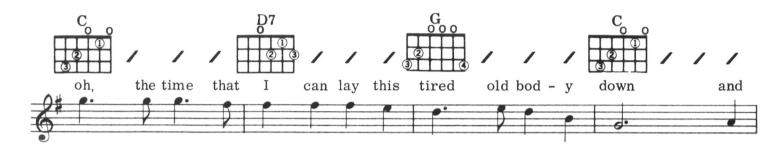

1. gain. There's gain. 2. And

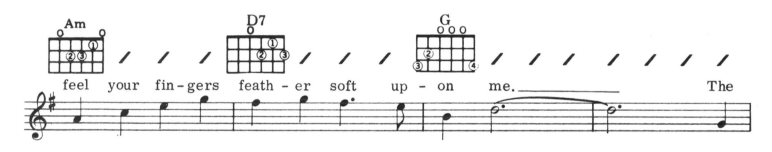

oh, the time that I can lay this tired old bod-y down and

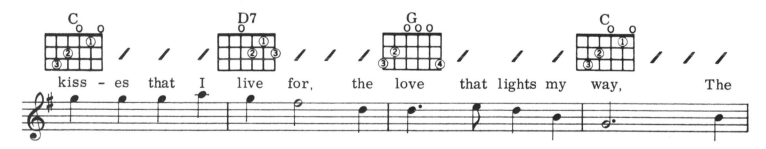

feel your fin-gers feath-er soft up-on me. The

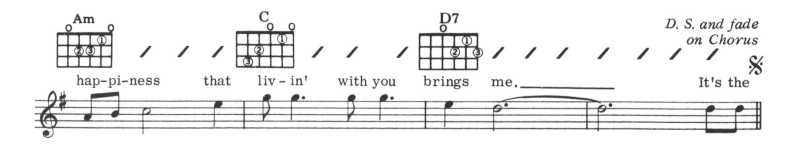

kiss-es that I live for, the love that lights my way, The

Am · C · D7 · *D. S. and fade on Chorus*

hap-pi-ness that liv-in' with you brings me. It's the

6

Calypso

Words and Music by
John Denver

Rather fast in 3 (or moderately slow in 1)

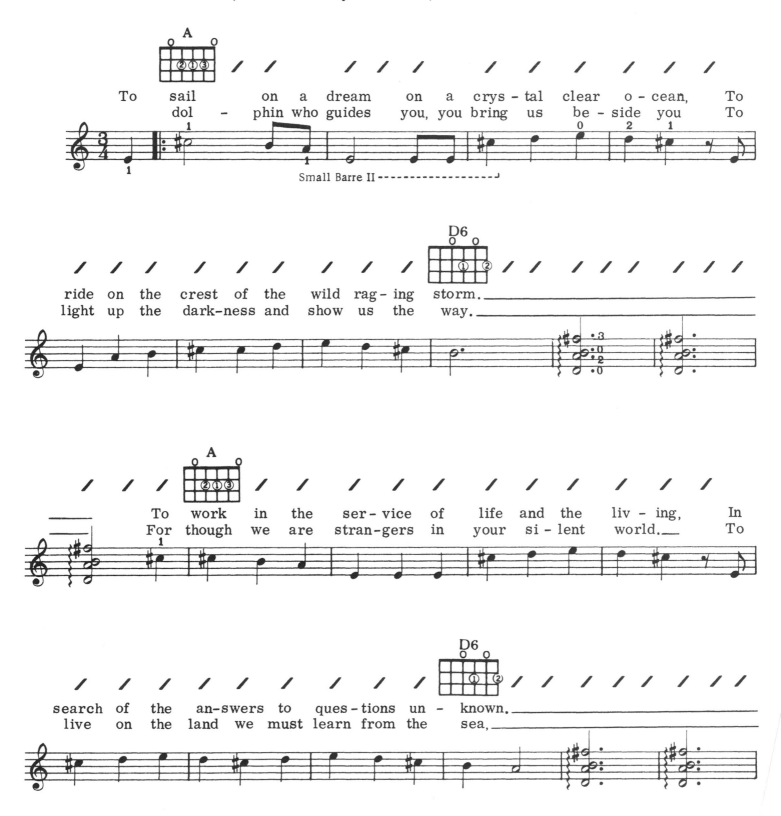

To be part of the move-ment and part of the grow-ing
To be true as the tide____ and free as a wind-swell,

Part of be-gin-ning to un-der-stand._____
Joy-ful and lov-ing in let-ting it be:_____

[Harmonics on 12th fret if desired.]

Aye,____ Ca-lyp-so, the plac-es you've

been to, The things that you've shown us, the sto-ries you

tell! Aye,____ Ca-lyp-so, I sing to your spir-it, The

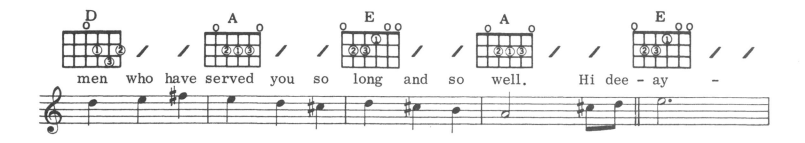

men who have served you so long and so well. Hi dee-ay -

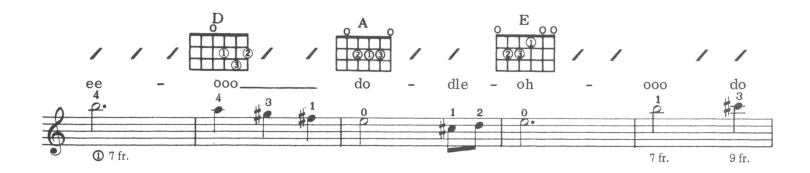

ee - ooo_____ do - dle - oh - ooo do

① 7 fr.   7 fr.   9 fr.

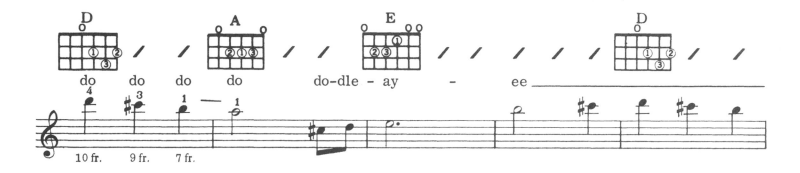

do do do do   do-dle - ay - ee _____

10 fr.   9 fr.   7 fr.

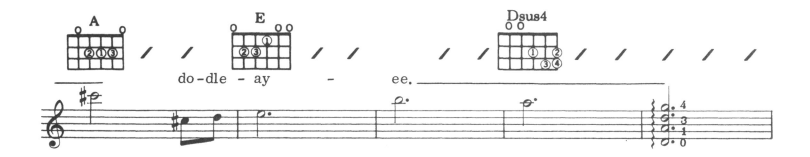

do-dle - ay - ee. _____

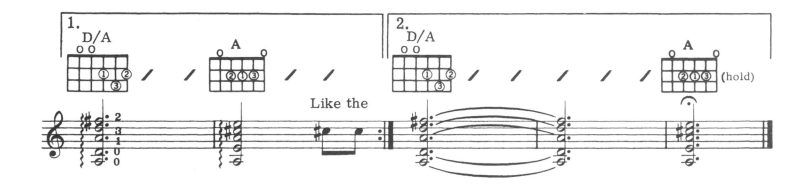

1.   2.

Like the

Eagles And Horses (I'm Flying Again)

Words by John Denver and Joe Henry
Music by John Denver

With a driving beat

1. Hors-es are crea-tures who wor-ship the earth.___ They gal-lop on feet of i-vo-ry. Con-strained by the won-der of dy-ing and birth, the hors-es still run, they are free.___ My bod-y is mere-ly the shell of my soul. But the flesh must be giv-en its due, like a po-ny that car-ries its rid-er back home,

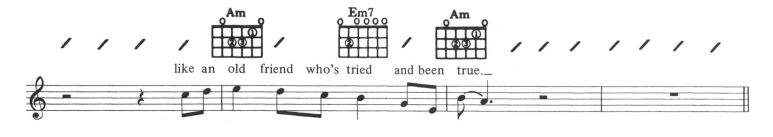

like an old friend who's tried and been true._

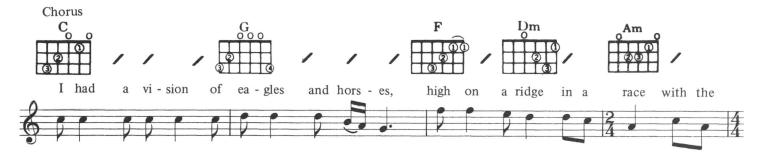

Chorus

I had a vi - sion of ea - gles and hors - es, high on a ridge in a race with the

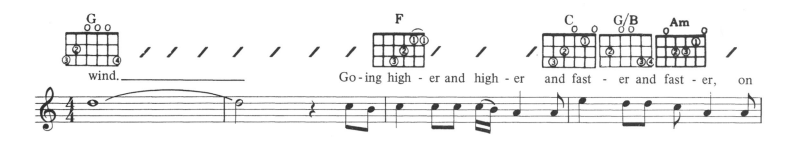

wind._____ Go - ing high - er and high - er and fast - er and fast - er, on

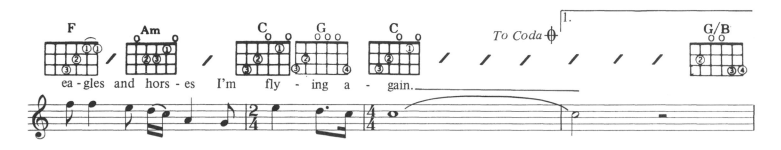

To Coda ⊕ 1.

ea - gles and hors - es I'm fly - ing a - gain._

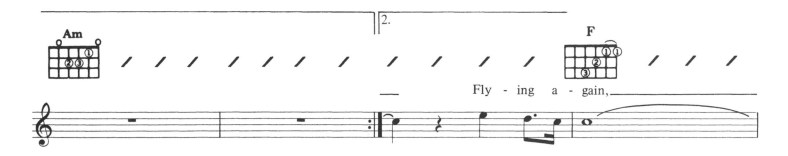

2.

Fly - ing a - gain,_____

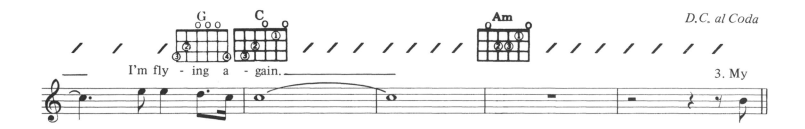

D.C. al Coda

I'm fly - ing a - gain._____   3. My

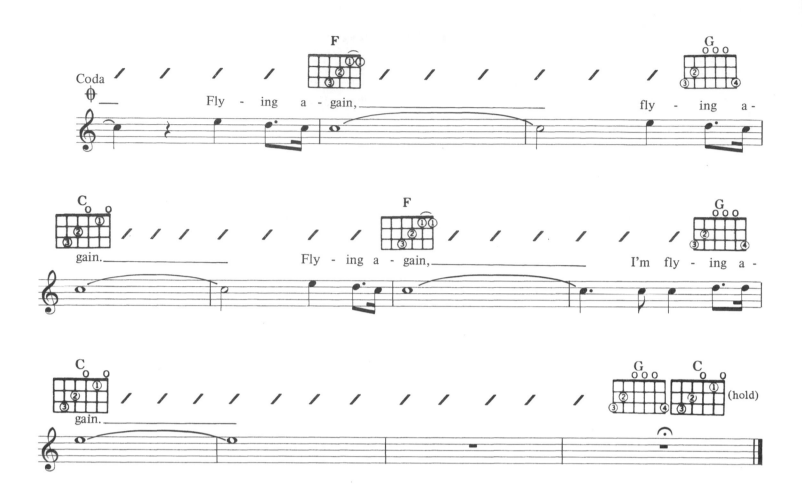

2. Eagles inhabit the heavenly heights;
   They know neither limit nor bound.
   They're the guardian angels of darkness and light;
   They see all and hear every sound.
   My spirit will never be broken or caught,
   For the soul is a free-flying thing,
   Like an eagle that needs neither comfort nor thought
   To rise up on glorious wings. *(To Chorus)*

3. My body is merely the shell of my soul,
   But the flesh must be given its due,
   Like a pony that carries its master back home,
   Like an old friend who's tried and been true.
   My spirit will never be broken or caught,
   For the soul is a free-flying thing,
   Like an eagle that needs neither comfort nor thought
   To rise up on glorious wings. *(To Chorus)*

Fly Away

Words and Music by
John Denver

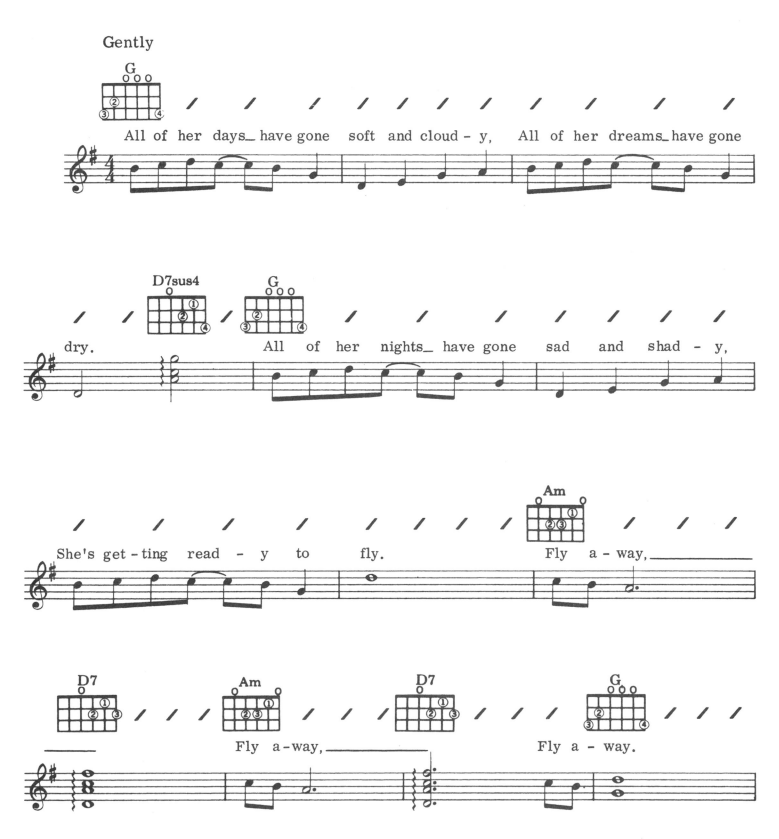

13

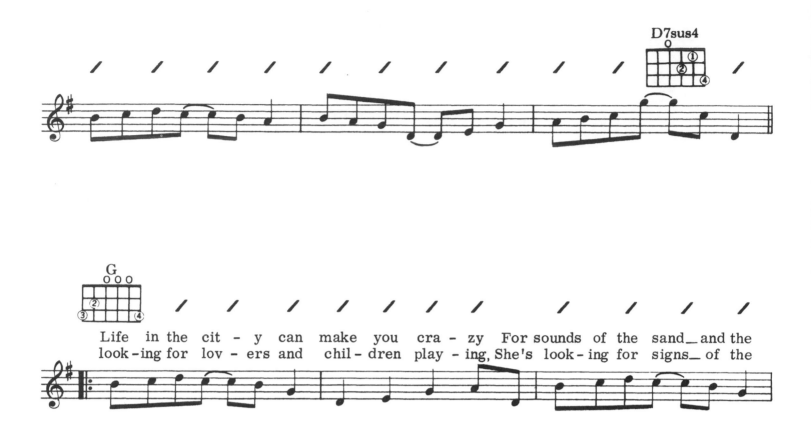

Life in the cit - y can make you cra - zy For sounds of the sand_ and the
look -ing for lov - ers and chil - dren play - ing, She's look -ing for signs_ of the

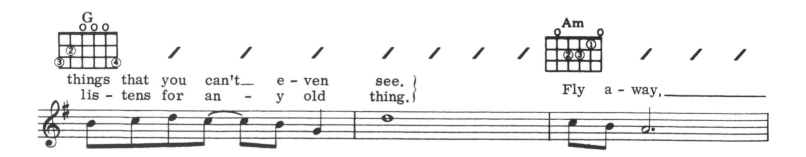

sea.   Life in a high - rise can make you hun - gry For
spring.   She lis-tens for laugh - ter and sounds of danc - ing, She

things that you can't_ e - ven see.)
lis - tens for an - y old thing.)

Fly a - way,_____

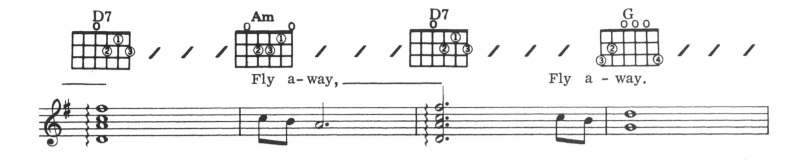

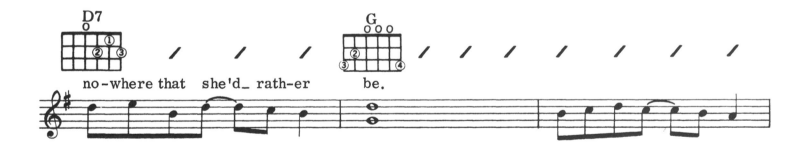

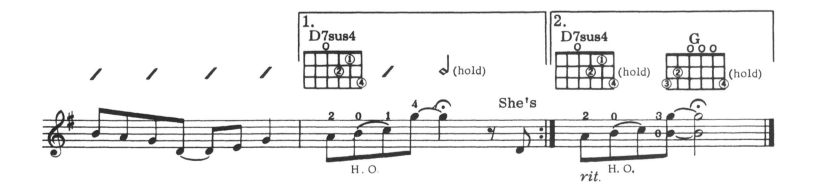

Follow Me

Words and Music by
John Denver

Moderately fast

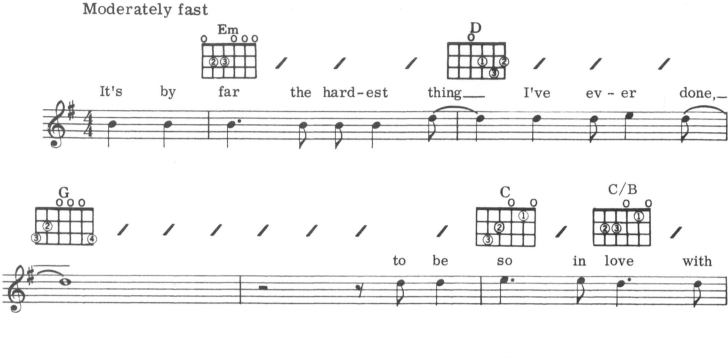

It's by far the hard-est thing__ I've ev-er done,__ to be so in love with you and so a - lone.

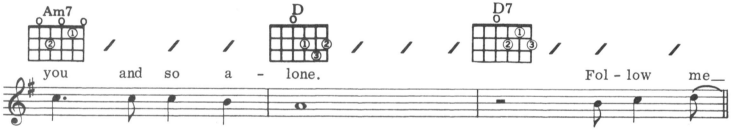

Fol-low me__

where I go,__ what I do__ and who I know,__

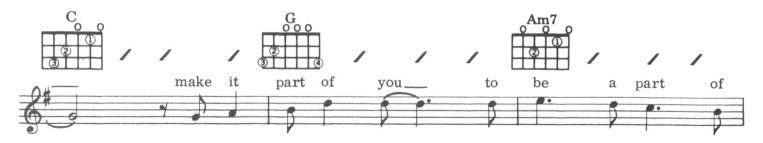

make it part of you__ to be a part of

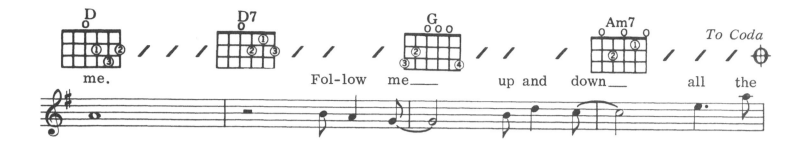

To Coda

me. Fol-low me___ up and down___ all the

way and all a-round,___ take my hand_ and say you'll fol-low me.__

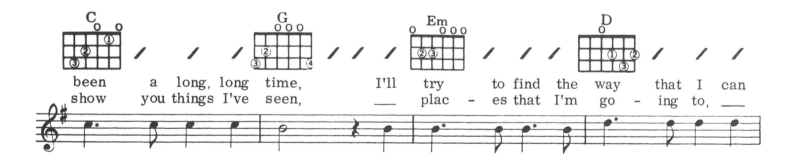

It's long been on my mind,___ you know it's
You see, I'd like to share my life___ with you and

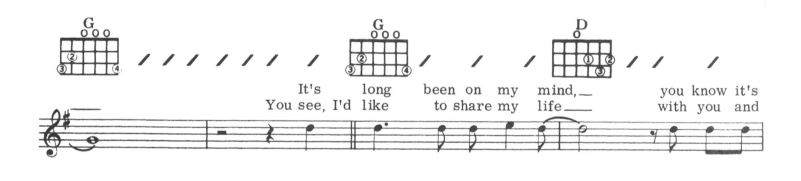

been a long, long time, I'll try to find the way that I can
show you things I've seen, ___ plac - es that I'm go - ing to, ___

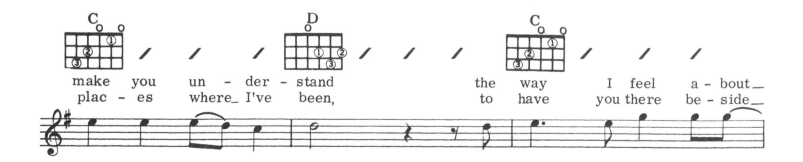

make you un - der - stand the way I feel a-bout___
plac - es where_ I've been, to have you there be - side___

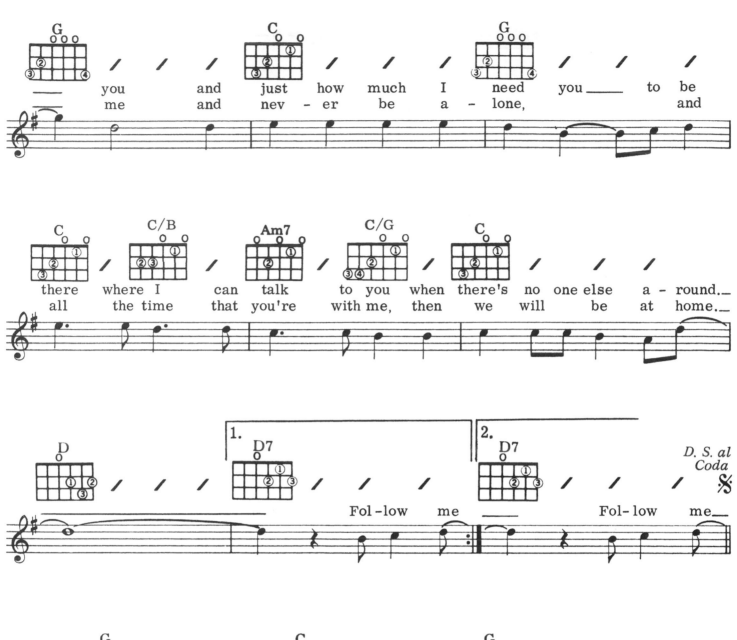

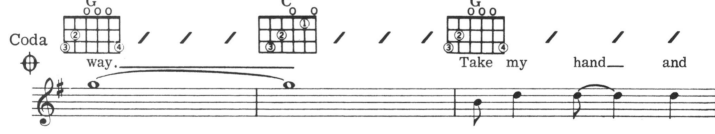

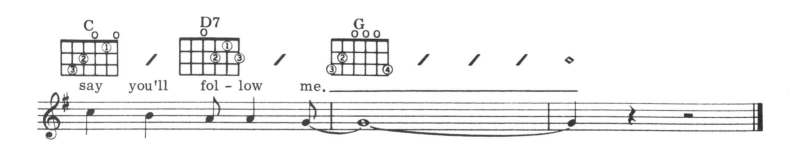

Leaving On A Jet Plane

Words and Music by
John Denver

ear - ly morn,__ the tax - i's wait-in', he's blow - in' his horn,__ al -
think of you,__ ev'ry song I sing I'll sing for you,__ when
days to come__ when I won't have to leave a - lone,__ a -

read - y I'm so lone - some I could die._____ So
I come back I'll bring your wed - ding ring._____ So
bout the times I won't have to say:_____ —

Chorus

kiss me and smile for me,__ tell me that__ you'll

wait for me,__ hold me like__ you'll nev - er let me

go._____ 'Cause I'm leav - in' on a jet__ plane,

For Baby (For Bobbie)

Words and Music by
John Denver

Slowly, in 2

I'll walk in the rain by your side,_____ I'll
(I'll) be there when you're feel-ing down_____ To

cling to the warmth of your hand,_____ I'll
kiss a-way the tears if you cry,_____ —

do an-y-thing to help you un-der-stand, I'll
I'll share with you ___ all the hap-pi-ness I've found, A re-

love you more than an-y-bod-y can._____ And the
flec-tion of the love___ in your eyes._____ And I'll

wind will whis-per your name to me,_____
sing you the songs of the rain-bow,_____ The

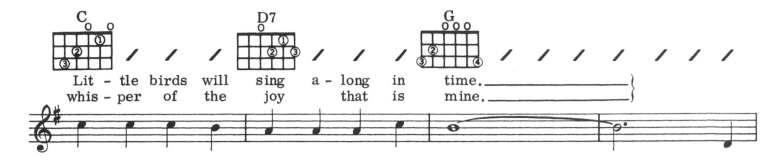

Lit - tle birds will sing a - long in time._____
whis - per of the joy that is mine._____

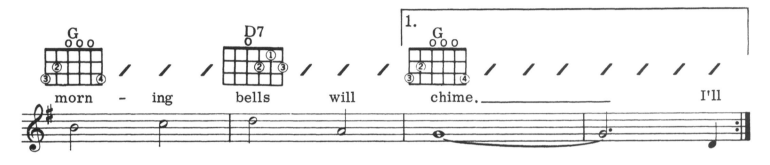

Leaves will bow down when you walk by And

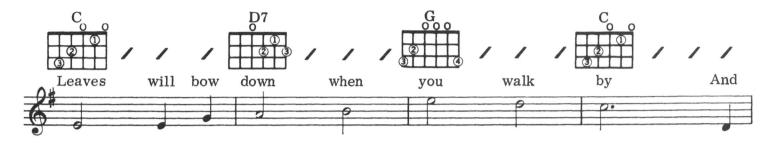

1.

morn - ing bells will chime._____ I'll

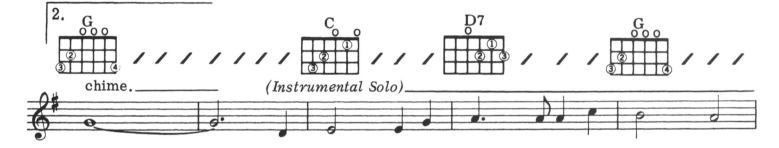

2.

chime._____ *(Instrumental Solo)*_____

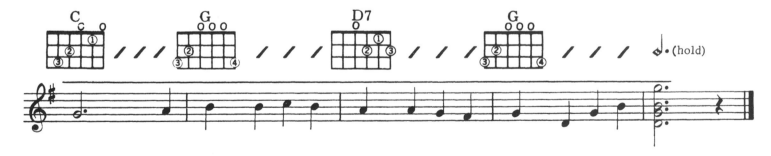

♩. (hold)

I'll walk in the rain by your side,
I'll cling to the warmth of your tiny hands.
I'll do anything to help you understand
And I'll love you more than anybody can.

And the wind will whisper your name to me,
Little birds will sing along in time.
Leaves will bow down when you walk by
And morning bells will chime.

For You

Words and Music by
John Denver

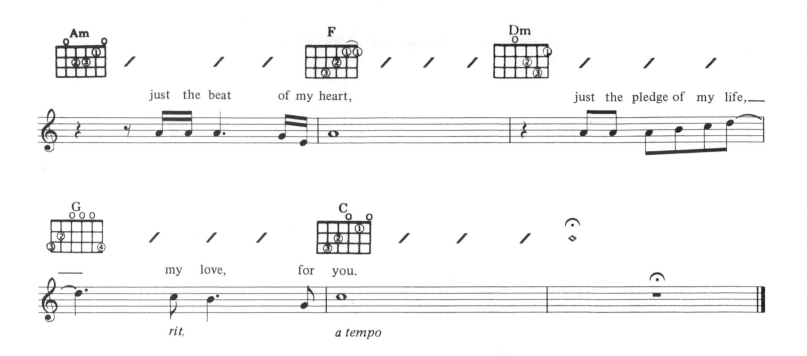

just the beat   of my heart,   just the pledge of my life,___

___ my love,   for   you.

rit.   *a tempo*

2. Just to sit by your window,
   Just to touch in the night,
   Just to offer a prayer each day for you.
   Just to long for your kisses,
   Just to dream of your sighs,
   Just to know that I'd give my life for you. *(To Chorus)*

3. Just to wake up each morning,
   Just to you by my side,
   Just to know that you're never really far away.
   Just a reason for living,
   Just to say I adore,
   Just to know that you're here in my heart to stay. *(To Chorus)*

Looking For Space

Words and Music by
John Denver

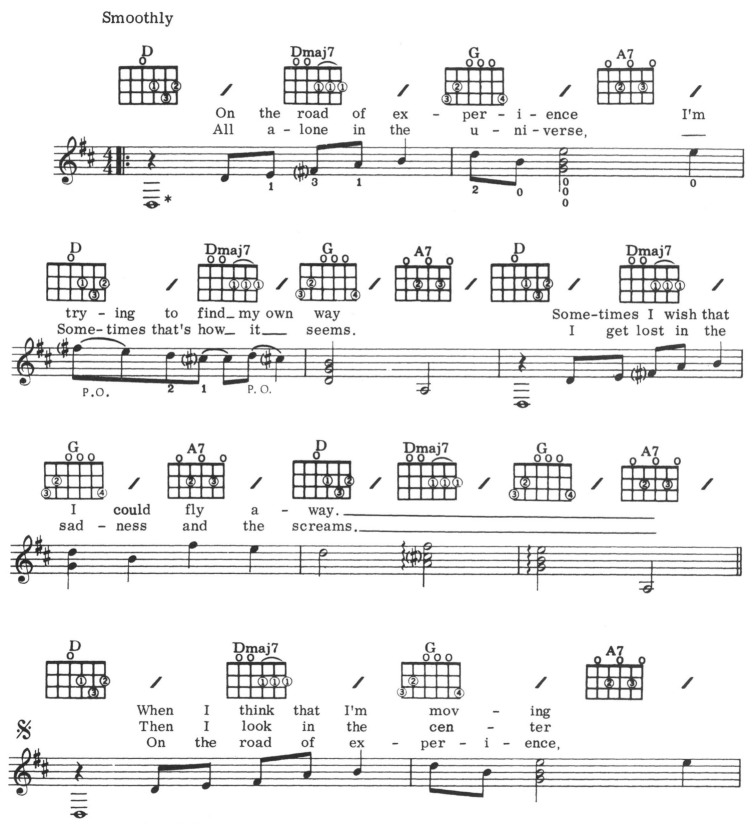

*Tune lowest string to D.

27

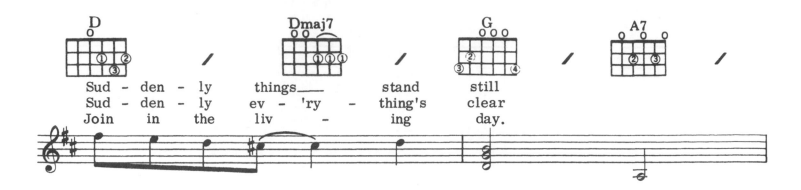

Sud - den - ly things___ stand still
Sud - den - ly ev - 'ry - thing's clear
Join in the liv - ing day.

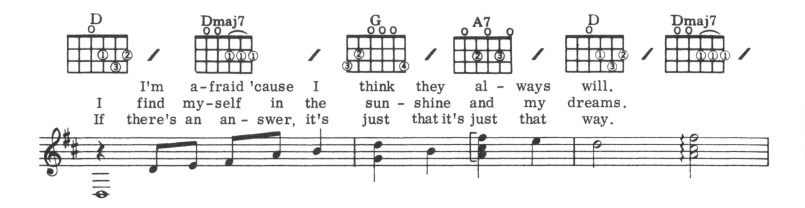

I'm a-fraid 'cause I think they al - ways will.
I find my-self in the sun - shine and my dreams.
If there's an an - swer, it's just that it's just that way.

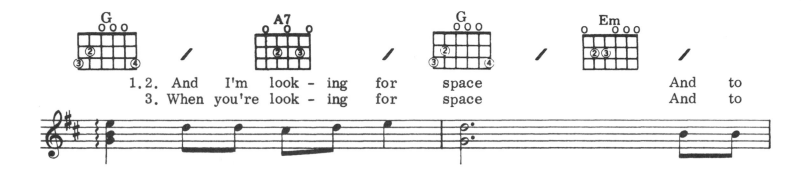

1.2. And I'm look - ing for space And to
3. When you're look - ing for space And to

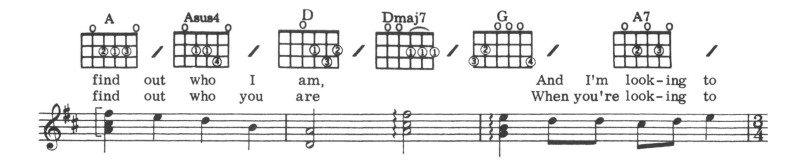

find out who I am, And I'm look-ing to
find out who you are When you're look-ing to

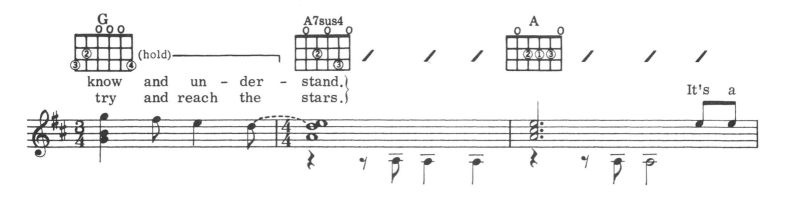

know and un - der - stand.)
try and reach the stars.)
It's a

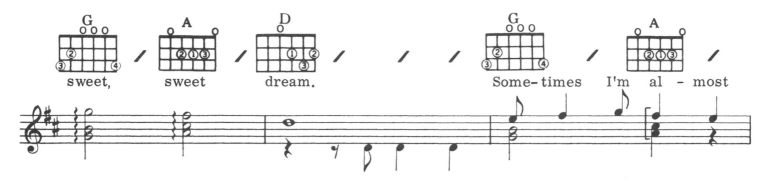

sweet, sweet dream. Some-times I'm al - most

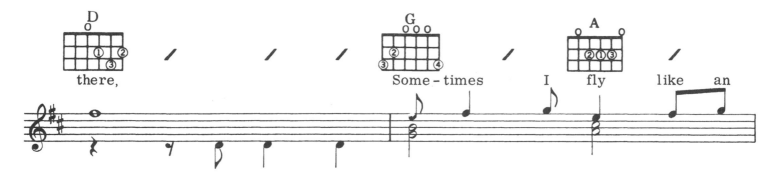

there, Some-times I fly like an

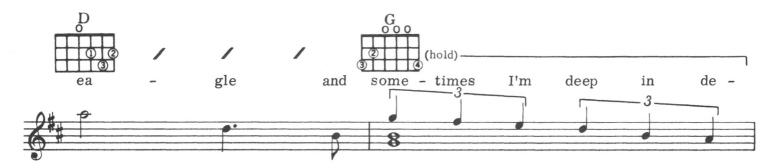

ea - gle and some - times I'm deep in de -

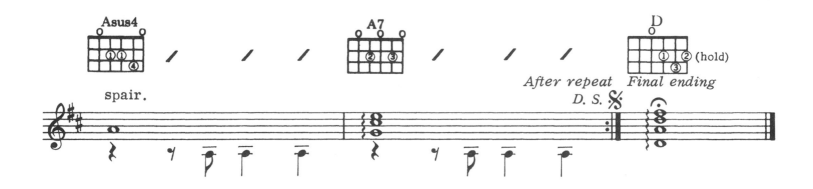

spair.

After repeat *Final ending*
D. S. %

Grandma's Feather Bed

Words and Music by
Jim Connor

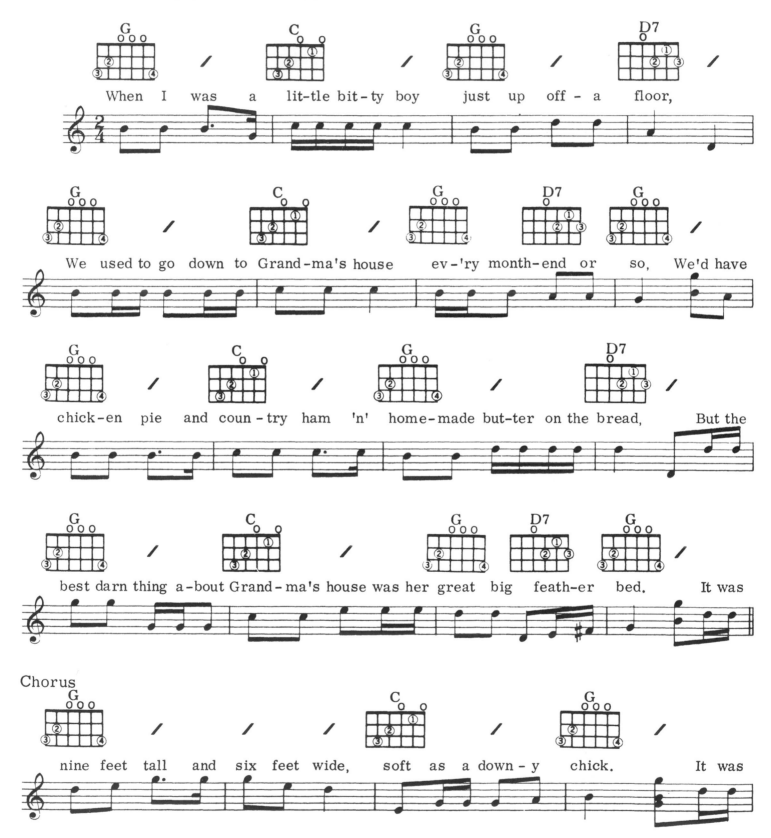

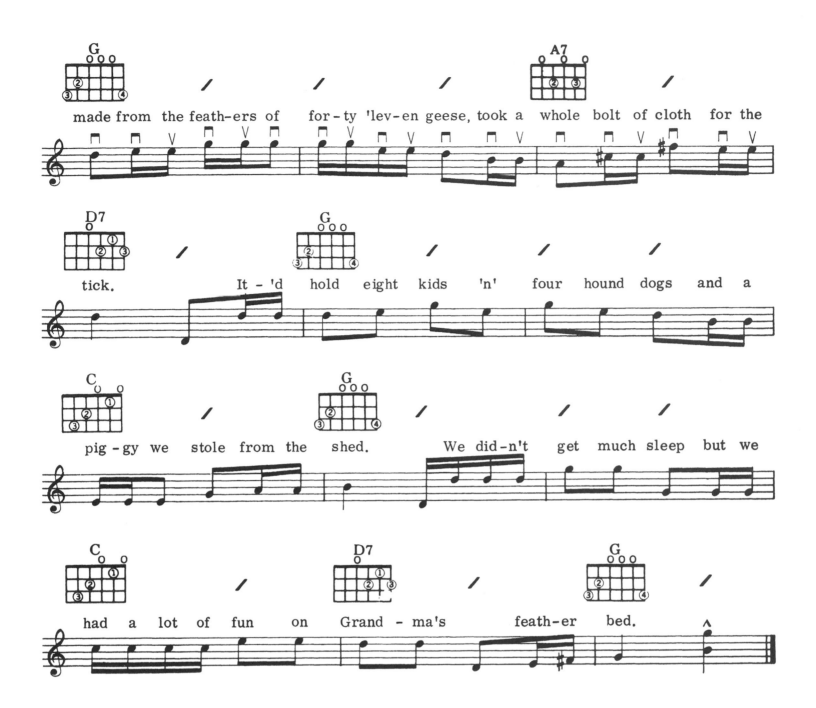

made from the feath-ers of for-ty 'lev-en geese, took a whole bolt of cloth for the tick. It-'d hold eight kids 'n' four hound dogs and a pig-gy we stole from the shed. We did-n't get much sleep but we had a lot of fun on Grand-ma's feath-er bed.

2. After supper we'd sit around the fire,
   The old folks'd spit and chew,
   Pa would talk about the farm and the war,
   And Granny'd sing a ballad or two.

   I'd sit and listen and watch the fire
   Till the cobwebs filled my head,
   Next thing I'd know I'd wake up in the mornin'
   In the middle of the old feather bed.
   (Chorus)

3. Well, I love my Ma, I love my Pa,
   I love Granny and Grandpa, too,
   I been fishin' with my uncle, rassled with my cousin,
   I even kissed Aunt Lou ooo!

   But if I ever had to make a choice,
   I guess it oughta be said
   That I'd trade 'em all plus the gal down the road
   For Grandma's feather bed.
   (Chorus)

I'm Sorry

Words and Music by
John Denver

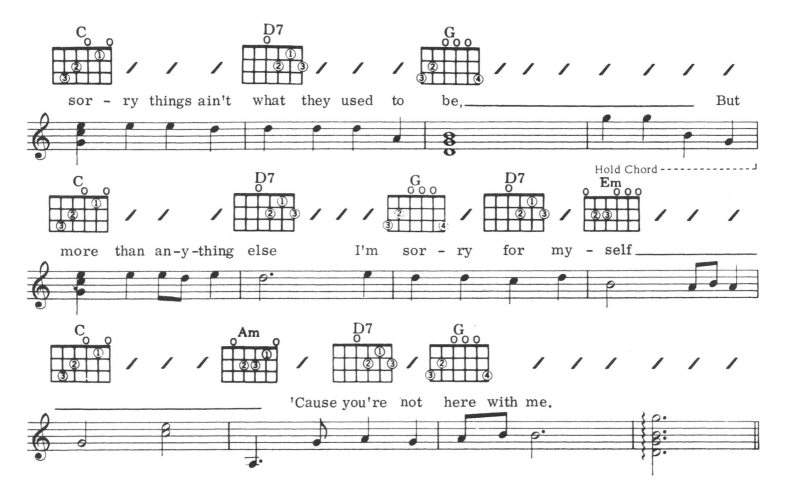

C, D7, G — sor - ry things ain't what they used to be,_____ But

Hold Chord - - - - - - - - -

C, D7, G, D7, Em — more than an-y-thing else I'm sor - ry for my - self_____

C, Am, D7, G — _____ 'Cause you're not here with me.

(Verse) Our friends all ask about you, I say you're doin' fine
I expect to hear from you almost anytime.
But they all know I'm cryin', that I can't sleep at night,
They all know I'm dyin' down deep inside.

(Chorus) I'm sorry for all the lies I told you,
I'm sorry for the things I didn't say,
But more than anything else I'm sorry for myself
I can't believe you went away.

(Chorus) I'm sorry if I took some things for granted,
I'm sorry for the chains I put on you,
But more than anything else I'm sorry for myself
For livin' without you.
(To Instrumental ending)

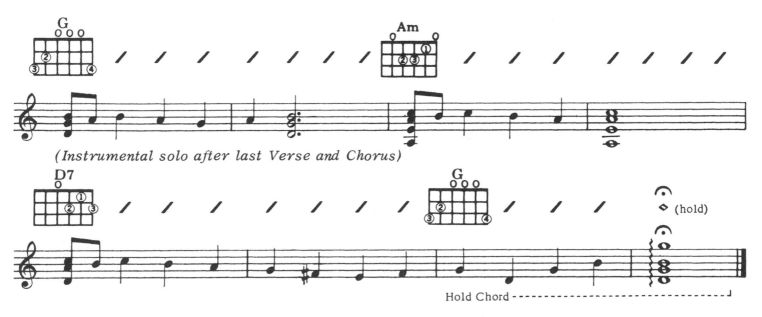

G, Am

(Instrumental solo after last Verse and Chorus)

D7, G — ◊ (hold)

Hold Chord -

My Sweet Lady

Words and Music by
John Denver

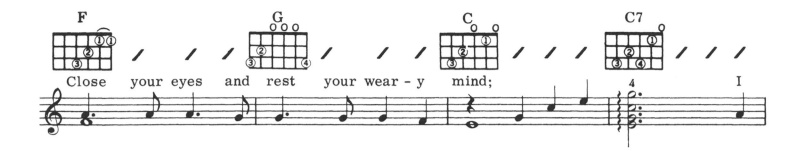

Close your eyes and rest your wear-y mind;   4   I

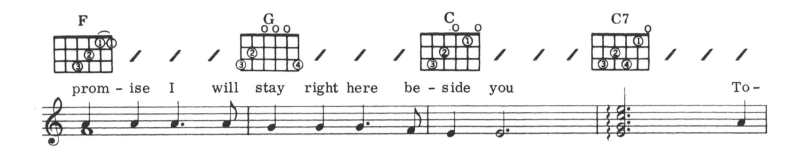

prom-ise I will stay right here be-side you   To-

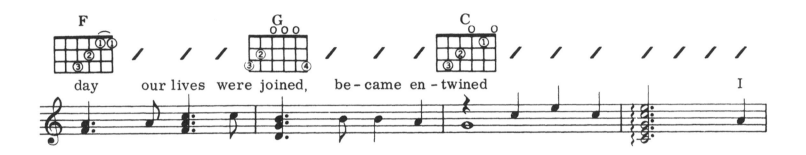

day our lives were joined, be-came en-twined   I

wish   that you could know   how much I love   you.   *D. C. for additional words*

2. Lady, are you happy, do you feel the way I do,
   Are there meanings that you've never seen before?
   Lady, my sweet lady, I just can't believe it's true
   And it's like I've never ever loved before.

   Close your eyes, *(etc.)*

3. *(same as 1st Verse)*

35

Never A Doubt

Words and Music by
John Denver

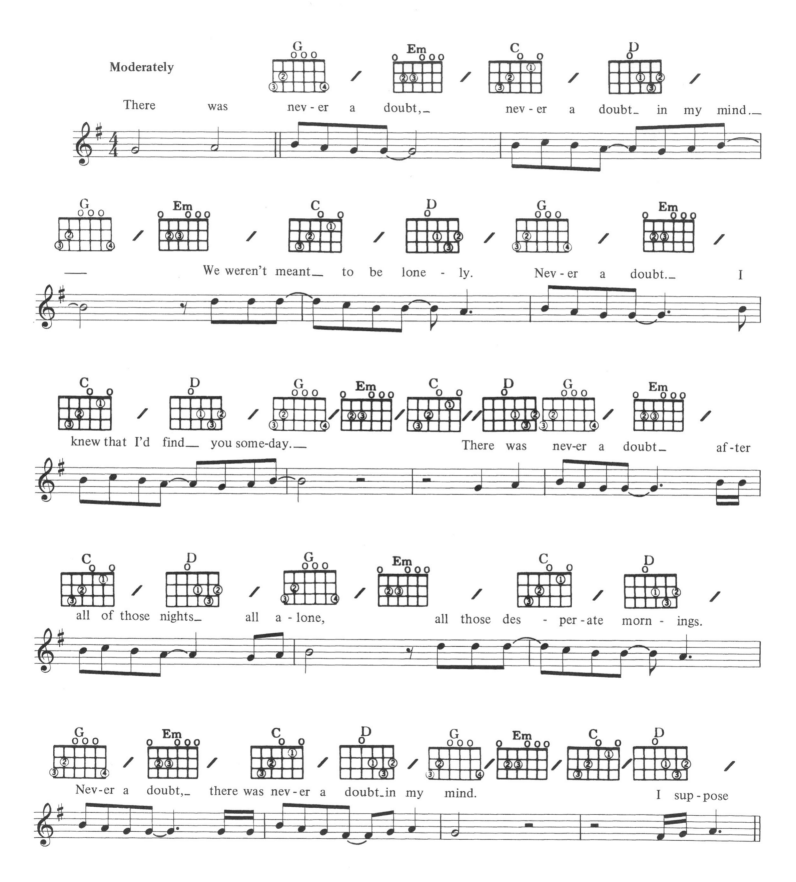

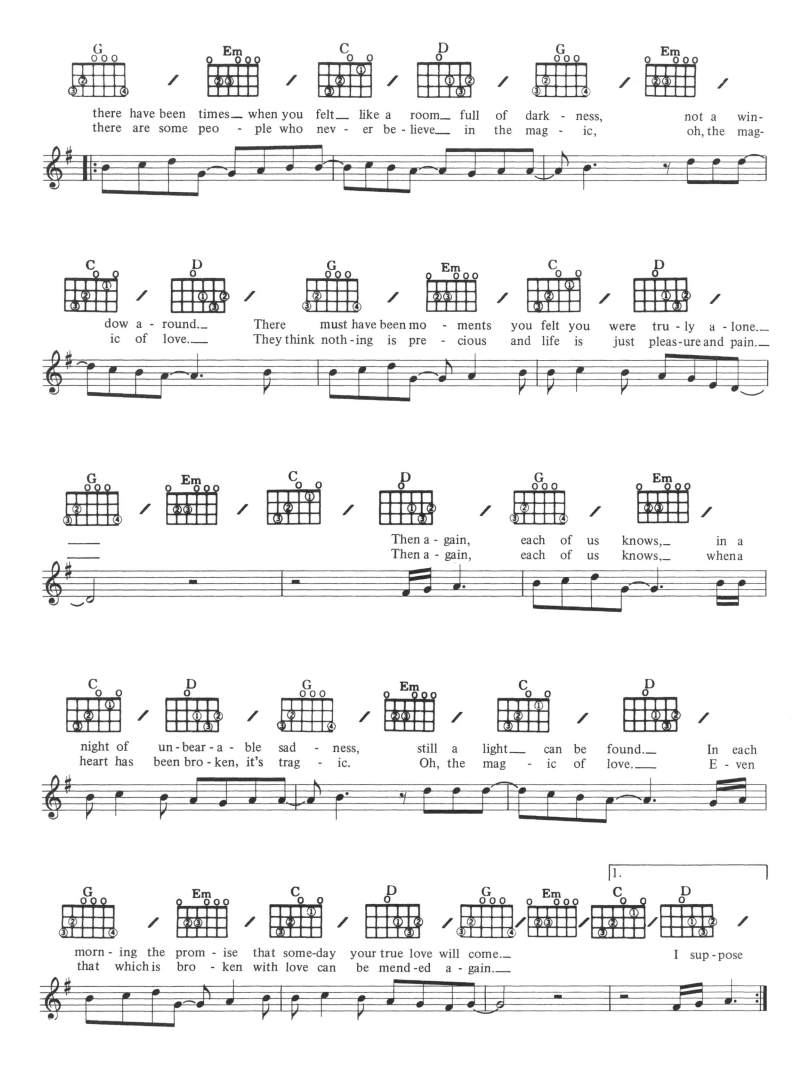

G   /   Em   /   C   /   D   /   G   /   Em   /

there have been times__ when you felt__ like a room__ full of dark - ness,   not a win-
there are some peo - ple who nev - er be - lieve__ in the mag - ic,   oh, the mag-

C   /   D   /   G   /   Em   /   C   /   D   /

dow a - round.__ There must have been mo - ments you felt you were tru - ly a - lone.__
ic of love.__ They think noth - ing is pre - cious and life is just pleas - ure and pain.__

G   /   Em   /   C   /   D   /   G   /   Em   /

__ Then a - gain, each of us knows,__ in a
__ Then a - gain, each of us knows,__ when a

C   /   D   /   G   /   Em   /   C   /   D   /

night of un - bear - a - ble sad - ness,   still a light__ can be found.__ In each
heart has been bro - ken, it's trag - ic.   Oh, the mag - ic of love.__ E - ven

1.

G   /   Em   /   C   /   D   /   G   Em   C   D   /

morn - ing the prom - ise that some - day your true love will come.__   I sup - pose
that which is bro - ken with love can be mend - ed a - gain.__

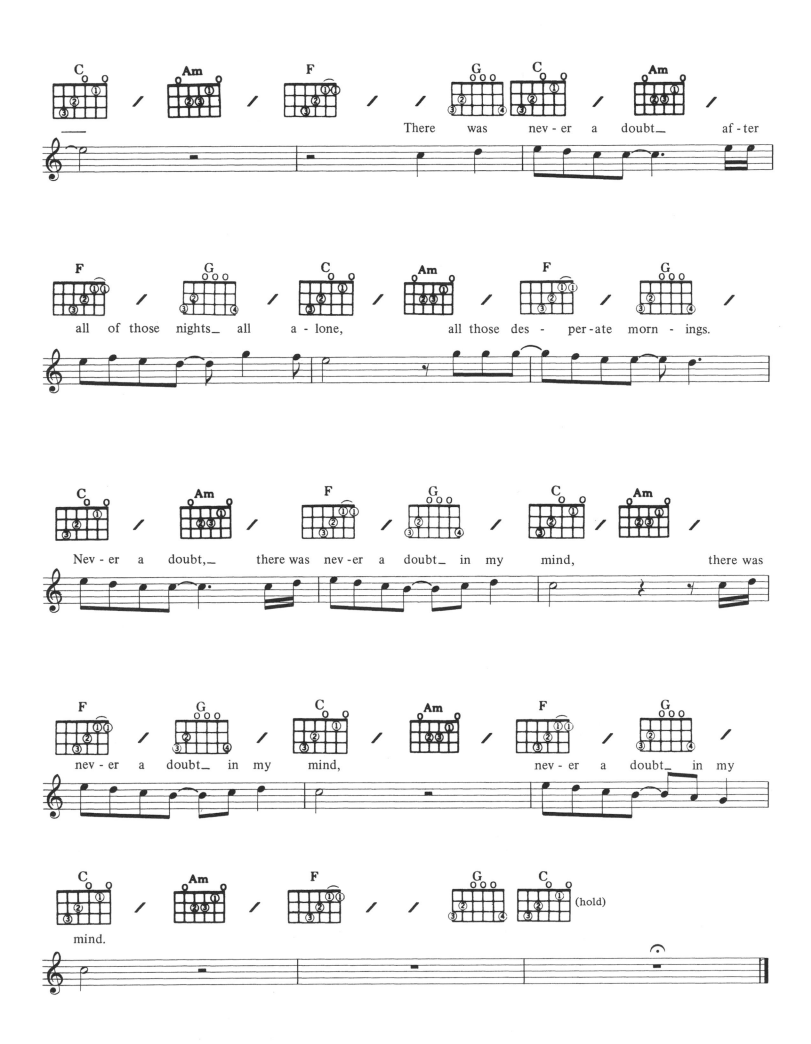

There was nev-er a doubt_ af-ter

all of those nights_ all a-lone, all those des-per-ate morn-ings.

Nev-er a doubt,_ there was nev-er a doubt_ in my mind, there was

nev-er a doubt_ in my mind, nev-er a doubt_ in my

mind.

Perhaps Love

Words and Music by
John Denver

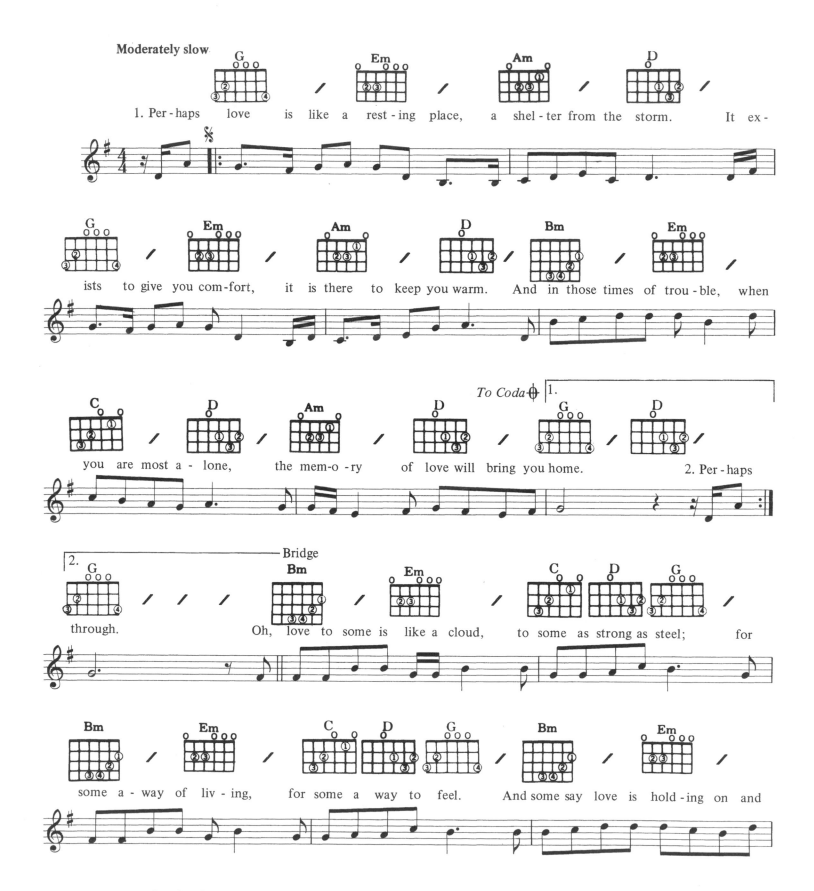

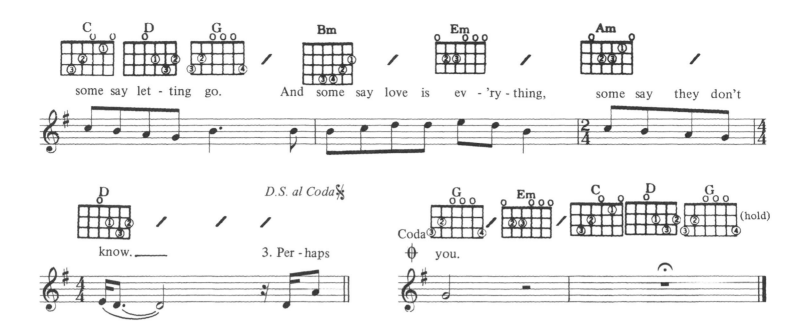

some say let - ting go.   And   some   say   love   is   ev - 'ry - thing,   some   say   they   don't

D.S. al Coda 𝄋

know._____   3. Per - haps   Coda   you.

2. Perhaps love is like a window, perhaps an open door.
It invites you to come closer, it wants to show you more.
And even if you lose yourself and don't know what to do,
The memory of love will see you through. *(To Bridge)*

3. Perhaps love is like the ocean, full of conflict, full of pain,
Like a fire when it's cold outside, thunder when it rains.
If you should live forever and all my dreams come true,
My memories of love will be of you.

Poems, Prayers And Promises

Words and Music by
John Denver

lieve in, how sweet it is to love some - one, how

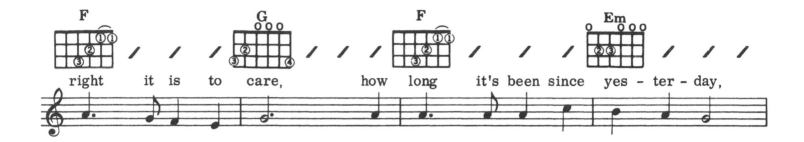

right it is to care, how long it's been since yes - ter - day,

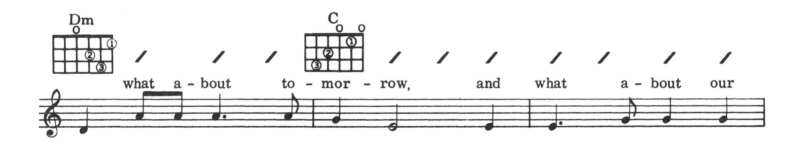

what a - bout to - mor - row, and what a - bout our

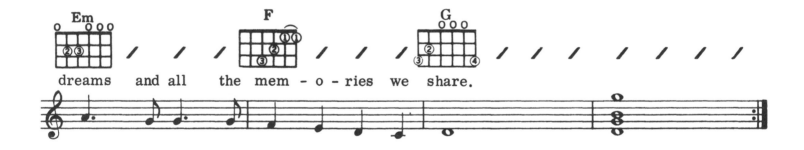

dreams and all the mem - o - ries we share.

Goodbye Again

Words and Music by
John Denver

Slowly, with a double time feeling

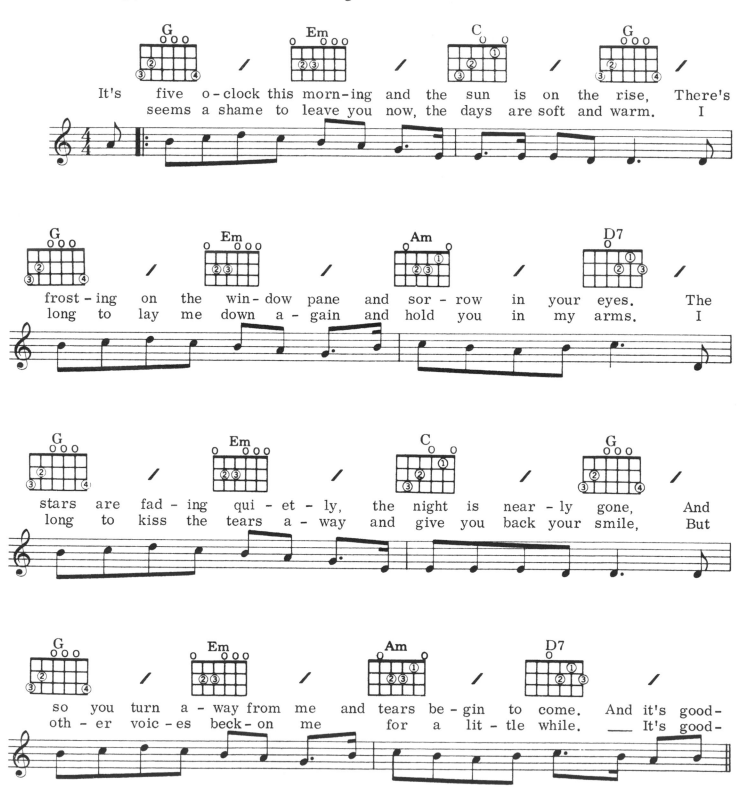

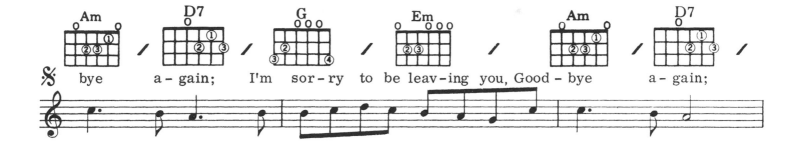

bye a - gain; I'm sor - ry to be leav - ing you, Good - bye a - gain;

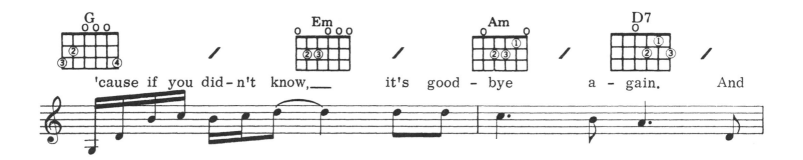

'cause if you did - n't know,___ it's good - bye a - gain. And

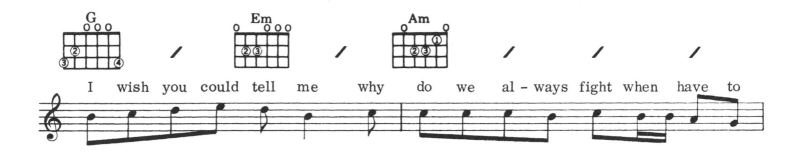

I wish you could tell me why do we al - ways fight when have to

1.

2. and Fine

go? 2. It go?___ 3. I have to go and see some friends of mine,

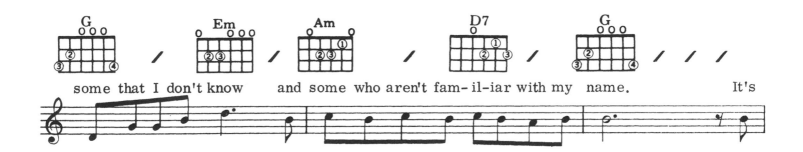

some that I don't know and some who aren't fam - il - iar with my name. It's

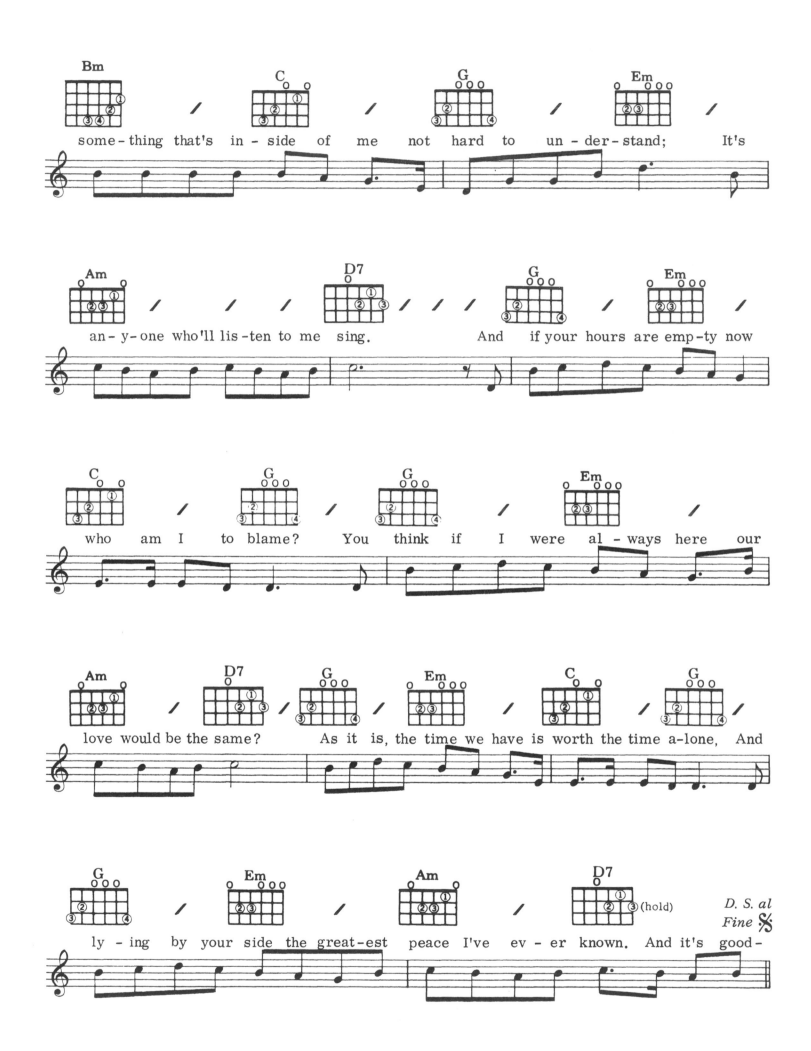

Rocky Mountain High

Words by John Denver
Music by John Denver and Mike Taylor

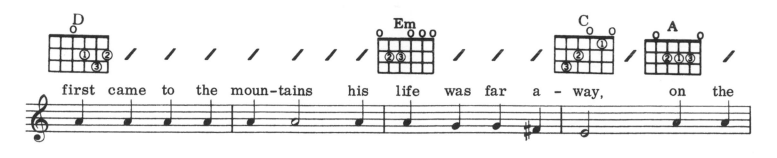

first came to the moun-tains his life was far a - way, on the

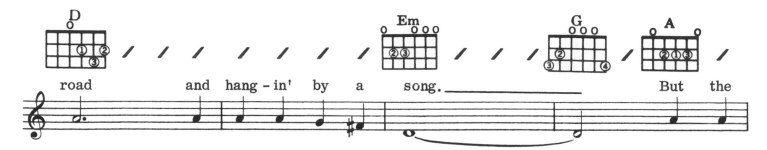

road and hang-in' by a song._____ But the

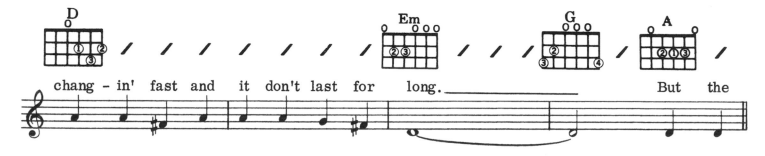

string's al-read-y brok-en and he does-n't real-ly care, it keeps

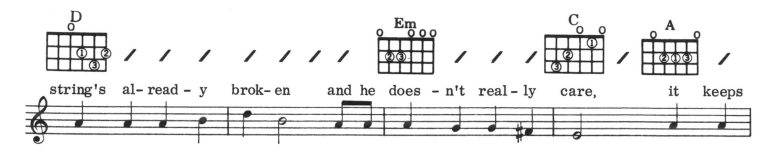

chang-in' fast and it don't last for long._____ But the

Chorus

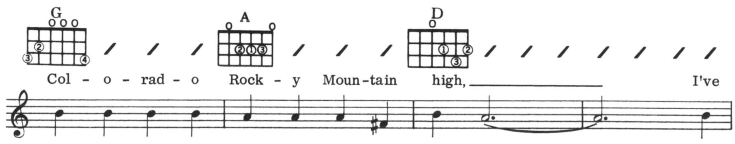

Col - o - rad - o Rock - y Moun-tain high,_____ I've

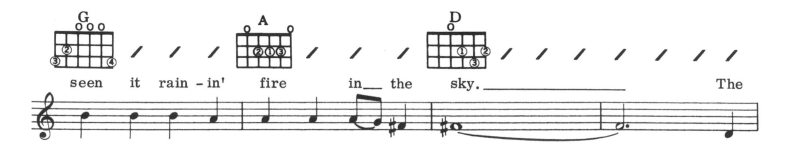

seen it rain-in' fire in__ the sky._____ The

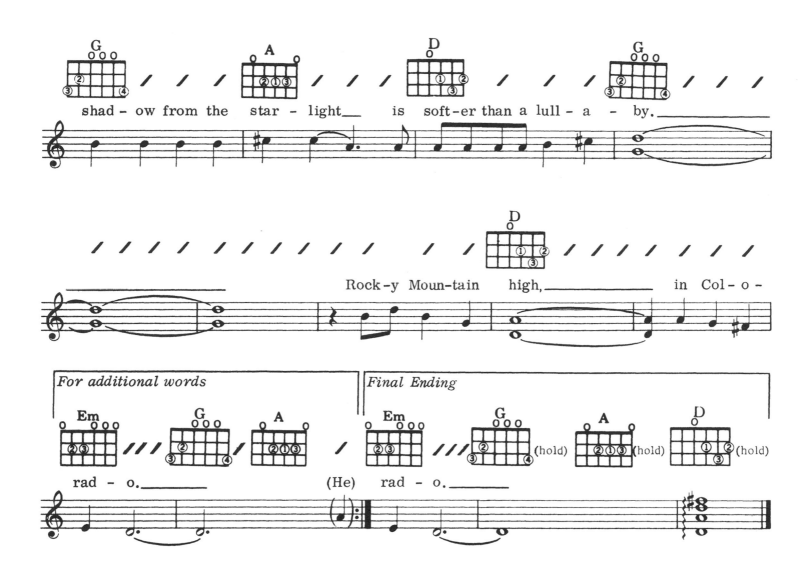

Verse 3. He climbed cathedral mountains, he saw silver clouds below,
He saw everything as far as you can see.
And they say that he got crazy once and he tried to touch the sun,
And he lost a friend but kept his memory.

Verse 4. Now he walks in quiet solitude, the forests and the streams
Seeking grace in every step he takes.
His sight has turned inside himself to try and understand
The serenity of a clear blue mountain lake.

Chorus 2. And the Colorado Rocky Mountain high,
I've seen it rainin' fire in the sky.
Talk to God and listen to the casual reply.
Rocky Mountain high in Colorado.

Verse 5. Now his life is full of wonder, but his heart still knows some fear
Of a simple thing he cannot comprehend.
Why they try to tear the mountains down to bring in a couple more,
More people, more scars upon the land.

Chorus 3. And the Colorado Rocky Mountain high,
I've seen it rainin' fire in the sky.
I know he'd be a poorer man if he never saw an eagle fly.
Rocky Mountain high.
It's a Colorado Rocky Mountain high (etc.)

Sunshine On My Shoulders

Words by John Denver
Music by John Denver,
Mike Taylor and Dick Kniss

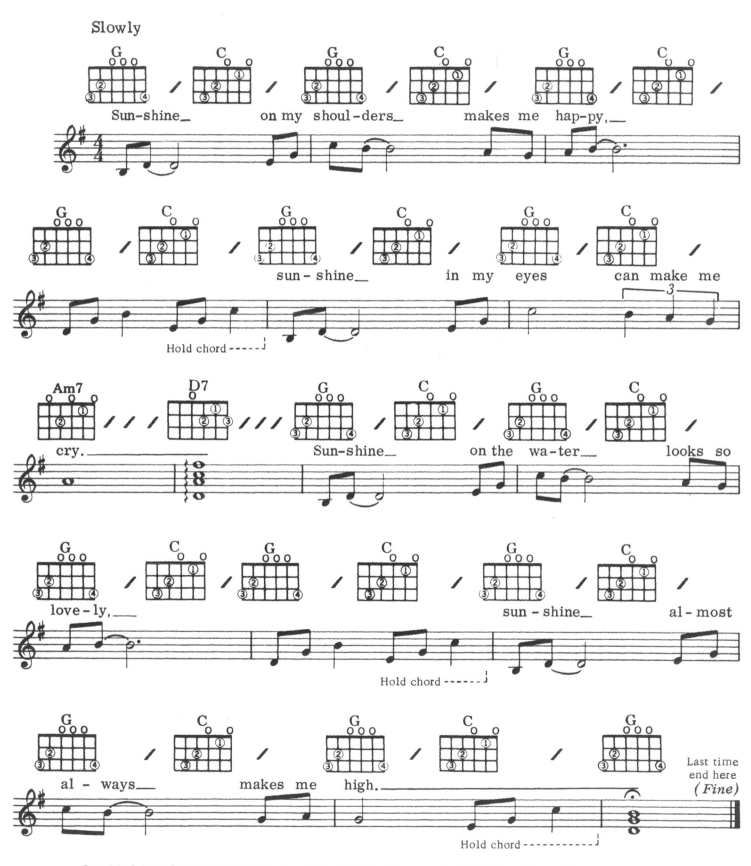

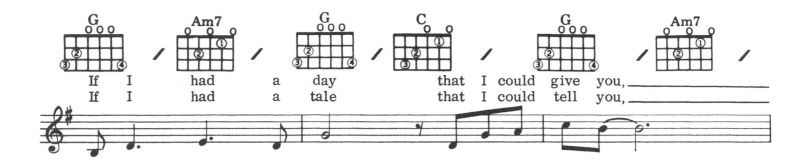

If I had a day that I could give you,
If I had a tale that I could tell you,

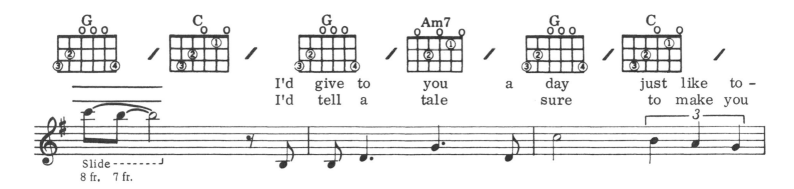

Slide - - - - - - -
8 fr.   7 fr.

I'd give to you a day just like to -
I'd tell a tale sure to make you

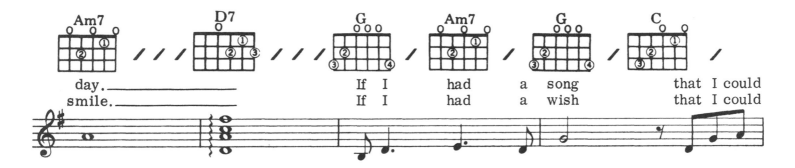

day.
smile.

If I had a song that I could
If I had a wish that I could

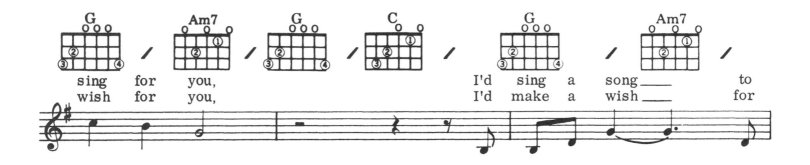

sing for you,
wish for you,

I'd sing a song to
I'd make a wish for

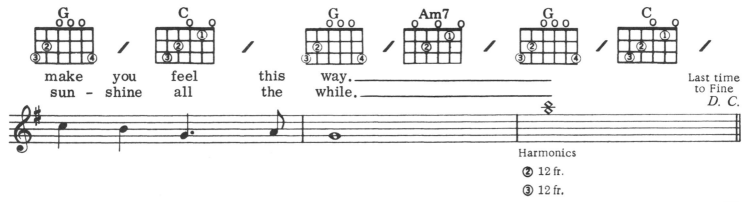

make you feel this way.
sun - shine all the while.

Last time
to Fine
D. C.

Harmonics
② 12 fr.
③ 12 fr.

Take Me Home, Country Roads

Words and Music by John Denver,
Bill Danoff and Taffy Nivert

Bright country tempo

Al-most heav — en, West Vir - gin - ia,
All my mem – 'ries gath - er 'round her,

Blue Ridge Moun - tains, Shen - an-do-ah Riv - er.____
min-er's la - dy, stran - ger to blue wa - ter.____

Life is old there, old - er than the trees,
Dark and dust - y, paint - ed on the sky,

young - er than the moun - tains grow - in' like a breeze.
mist - y taste of moon - shine, tear - drop in my eye.

Chorus

Coun - try roads,_____ take_ me home_____ to the

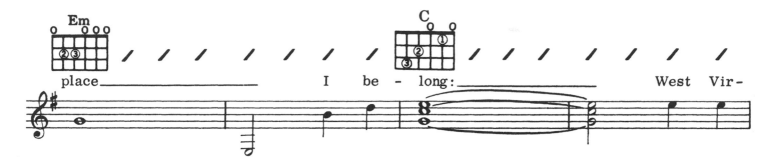

place_____ I be - long:_____ West Vir-

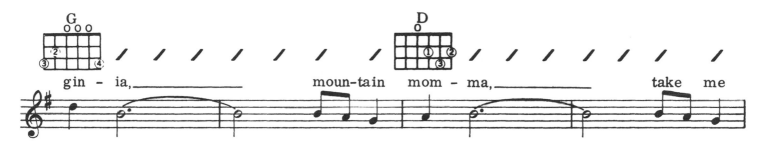

gin - ia,_____ moun-tain mom - ma,_____ take me

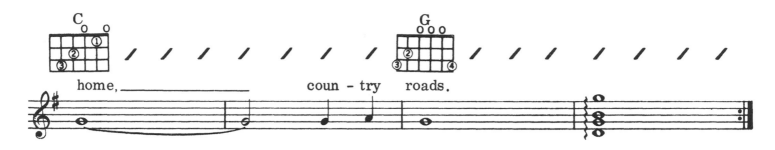

home,_____ coun - try roads.

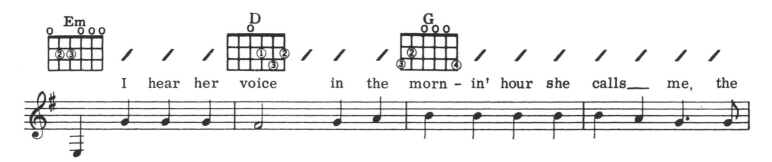

I hear her voice in the morn - in' hour she calls___ me, the

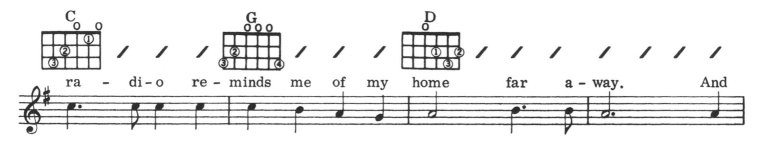

ra - di - o re - minds me of my home far a - way. And

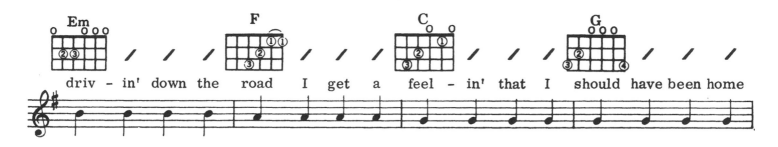

driv - in' down the road I get a feel - in' that I should have been home

yes - ter - day,_____ yes - ter - day._____

Chorus

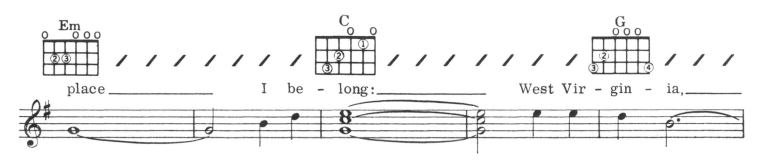

Coun - try roads,_____ take me home _____ to the

place _____ I be - long:_____ West Vir - gin - ia,_____

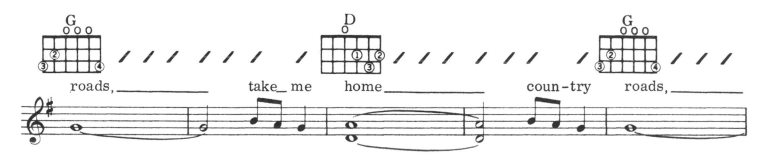

____ moun - tain mom - ma,_____ take_ me home _____ coun - try

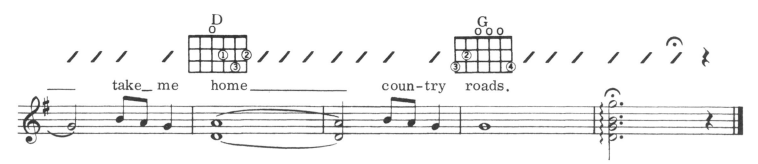

roads,_____ take_ me home_____ coun - try roads,_____

take_ me home_____ coun - try roads.

56

Whispering Jesse

Words and Music by
John Denver

57

I dreamed I left there on an old pal-o-

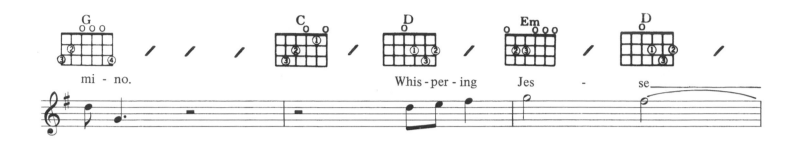

mi-no. Whis-per-ing Jes - se_____

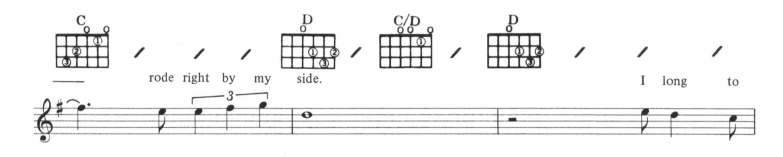

____ rode right by my side. I long to

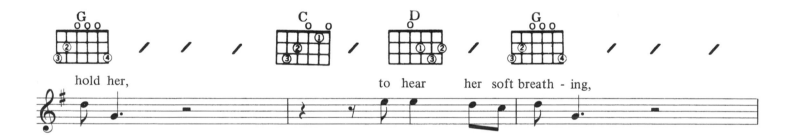

hold her, to hear her soft breath-ing,

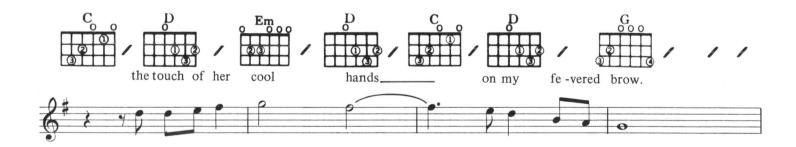

the touch of her cool hands_____ on my fe-vered brow.

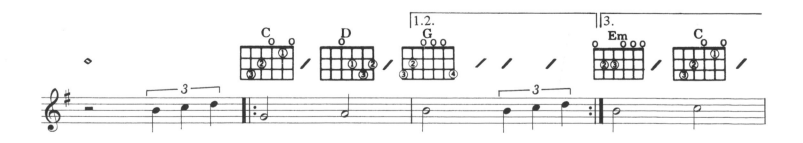

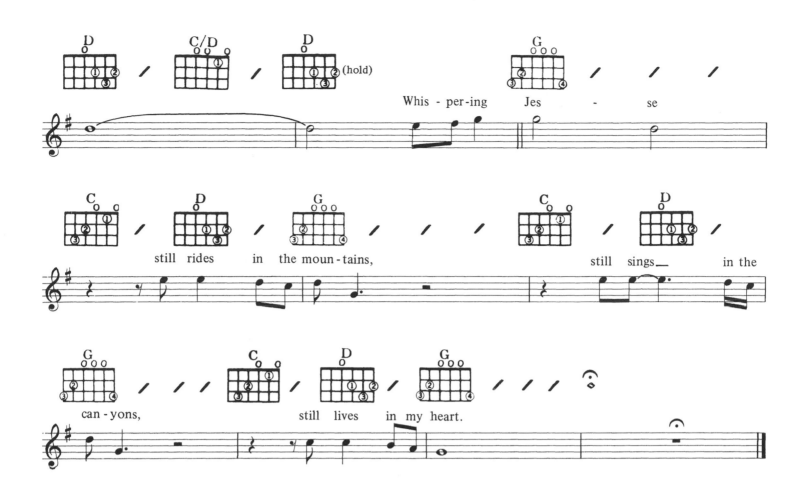

Whis-per-ing Jes - se still rides in the moun-tains, still sings__ in the can-yons, still lives in my heart.

2. I've always loved springtime, the passing of winter,
   The green of the new leaves and life goin' on,
   The promise of morning, the long days of summer,
   Warm nights of loving her beneath the bright stars.

3. I'm just an old cowboy from high Colorado,
   Too old to ride anymore, too blind to see.
   I sleep in the city now, away from my mountains,
   Away from the cabin we always called home.

Thank God I'm A Country Boy

Words and Music by
John Martin Sommers

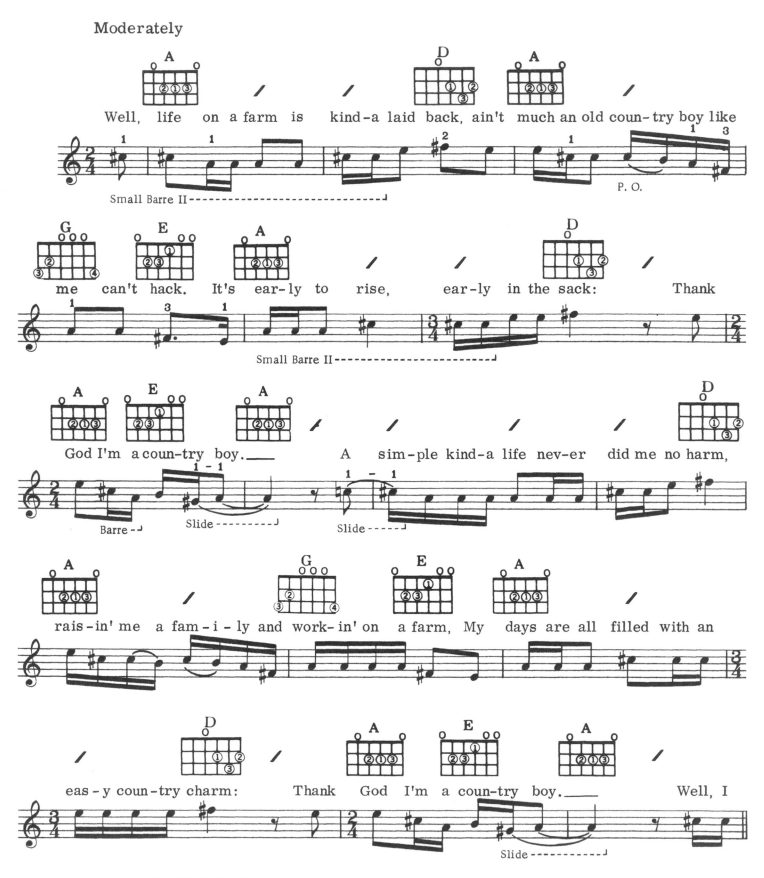

Chorus

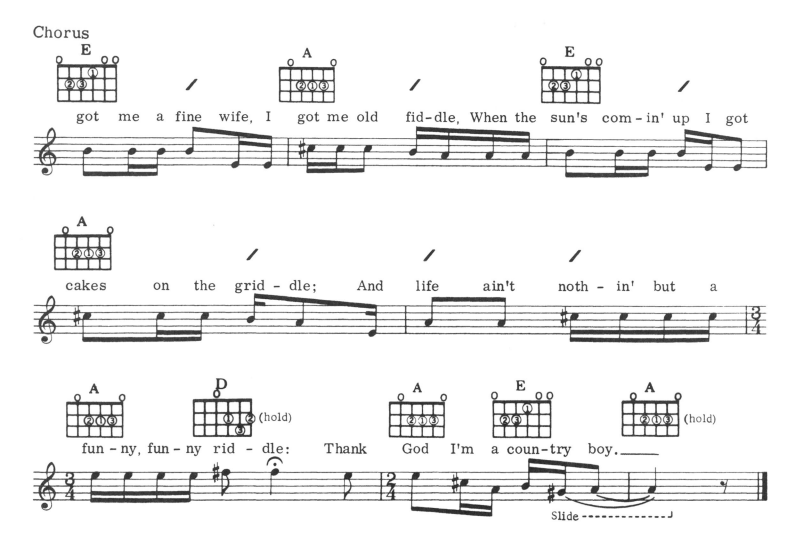

got me a fine wife, I got me old fid-dle, When the sun's com-in' up I got

cakes on the grid-dle; And life ain't noth-in' but a

fun-ny, fun-ny rid-dle: Thank God I'm a coun-try boy.____

Slide ------------

When the work's all done and the sun's settin' low
I pull out my fiddle and I rosin up the bow.
But the kids are asleep so I keep it kinda low:
Thank God I'm a country boy.
I'd play "Sally Goodin' " all day if I could,
But the Lord and my wife wouldn't take it very good.
So I fiddle when I can and I work when I should:
Thank God I'm a country boy.
(Chorus)

I wouldn't trade my life for diamonds or jewels,
I never was one of them money hungry fools.
I'd rather have my fiddle and my farmin' tools:
Thank God I'm a country boy.
Yeah, city folk drivin' in a black limousine,
A lotta sad people thinkin' that's mighty keen.
Well folks, let me tell you now exactly what I mean:
I thank God I'm a country boy.
(Chorus)

Well, my fiddle was my daddy's till the day he died,
And he took me by the hand and held me close to his side.
He said, "Live a good life and play my fiddle with pride,
And thank God you're a country boy."
My daddy taught me young how to hunt and how to whittle,
He taught me how to work and play a tune on the fiddle.
He taught me how to love and how to give just a little:
Thank God I'm a country boy.
(Chorus)

Wild Montana Skies

Words and Music by
John Denver

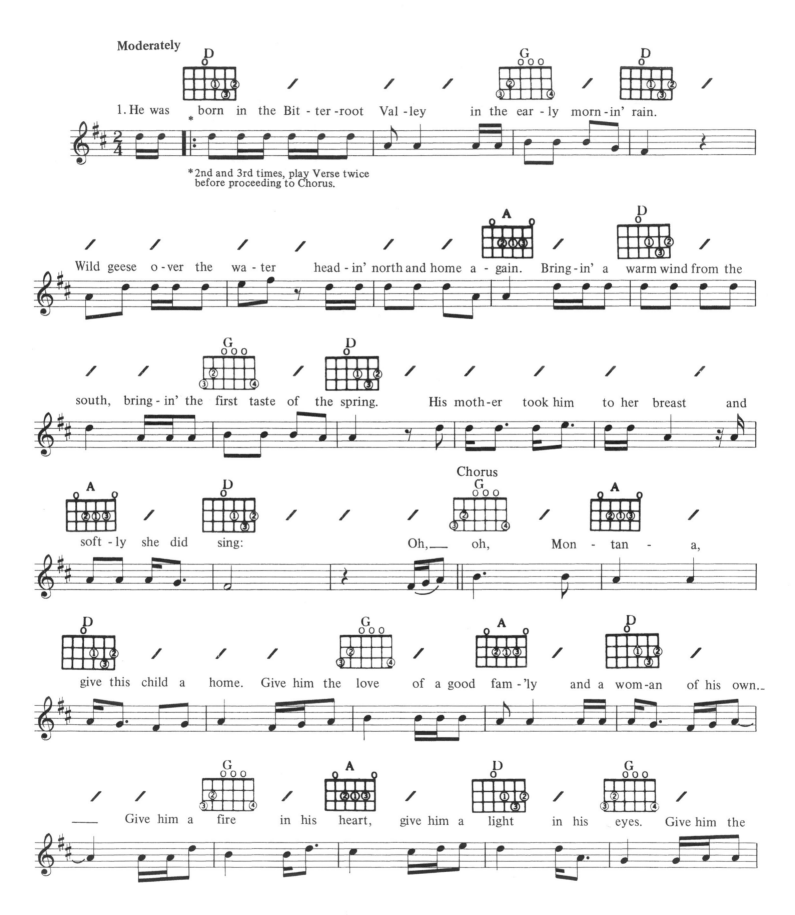

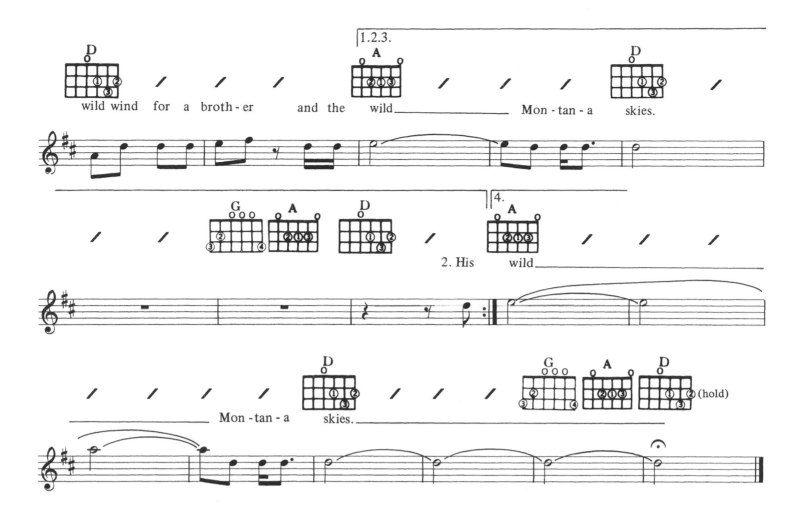

wild wind for a broth-er and the wild_____ Mon-tan-a skies.

2. His wild_____

_____ Mon-tan-a skies._____ (hold)

2. His mother died that summer, he never learned to cry.
   He never knew his father, he never did ask why.
   And he never knew the answers that would make an easy way.
   But he learned to know the wilderness and to be a man that way.

3. His mother's brother took him in to his family and his home,
   Gave him a hand that he could lean on and a strength to call his own.
   And he learned to be a farmer, and he learned to love the land,
   And he learned to read the seasons, and he learned to make a stand. *(To Chorus)*

4. On the eve of his twenty-first birthday he set out on his own.
   He was thirty years and runnin' when he found his way back home.
   Ridin' a storm across the mountains and an achin' in his heart,
   Said he came to turn the pages and to make a brand-new start.

5. Now, he never told the story of the time that he was gone.
   Some say he was a lawyer, some say he was a john.
   There was somethin' in the city that he said he couldn't breathe,
   And there was somethin' in the country that he said he couldn't leave. *(To Chorus)*

6. Now, some say he was crazy, some are glad he's gone.
   But some of us will miss him and we'll try to carry on.
   Giving a voice to the forest, giving a voice to the dawn,
   Giving a voice to the wilderness and the land that he lived on. *(To Chorus)*

Cherry Lane
Music

• *Quality In Printed Music* •